SAFE

ONLINE

PowerKiDS
press

New York

ROSEMARY JENNINGS

Published in 2017 by The Rosen Publishing Group, Inc.
29 East 21st Street, New York, NY 10010

First Edition

Editor: Theresa Morlock
Book Design: Reann Nye

Photo Credits: Cover (background) Photographee.eu/Shutterstock.com; cover (girl), p. 1 I love photo/Shutterstock.com; p. 5 wavebreakmedia/Shutterstock.com; p. 6 BestPhotoStudio/Shutterstock.com; p. 9 bikeriderlondon/Shutterstock.com; p. 10 Mango Productions/Corbis/Getty Images; p. 13 Yuganov Konstantin/Shutterstock.com; p. 14 Uber Images/Shutterstock.com; p. 17 Kdonmuang/Shutterstock.com; p. 18 Monkey Business Images/Shutterstock.com; p. 21 Lane Oatey/Blue Jean Images/Getty Images; p. 22 kryzhov/Shutterstock.com; p. 24 (computer) Petinov Sergey Mihilovich/Shutterstock.com; p. 24 (online) Denys Prykhodov/Shutterstock.com.

Library of Congress Cataloging-in-Publication Data

Names: Jennings, Rosemary, author.
Title: Safe online / Rosemary Jennings.
Description: New York : PowerKids Press, [2017] | Series: Safety smarts |
  Includes index.
Identifiers: LCCN 2016029139| ISBN 9781499427837 (pbk. book) | ISBN
  9781508153030 (6 pack) | ISBN 9781499429985 (library bound book)
Subjects: LCSH: Internet and children–Juvenile literature. |
  Internet–Security measures–Juvenile literature. | Online
  etiquette–Juvenile literature.
Classification: LCC HQ784.I58 J46 2017 | DDC 004.67/8083–dc23
LC record available at https://lccn.loc.gov/2016029139

Manufactured in the United States of America

CPSIA Compliance Information: Batch #BW17PK: For Further Information contact Rosen Publishing, New York, New York at 1-800-237-9932

CONTENTS

We have a **computer**.

5

We are safe **online**.

First, we tell our dad.

9

Dad goes online with us.

We do not talk to strangers online.

14

Strangers may lie to us.

We do not use our real names.

17

18

We use made-up names.

We are nice to others.

20

22

We stay safe online!

WORDS TO KNOW

computer

online

INDEX

WEBSITES

Due to the changing nature of Internet links, PowerKids Press has developed an online list of websites related to the subject of this book. This site is updated regularly. Please use this link to access the list:
www.powerkidslinks.com/safe/onli

24